WELCOME TO THE FAMILY

Copyright ©Elsa Kurt ISBN: 978-1-7346458-5-9

All rights reserved. No part of this publication may be reproduced, distributed, or transmitted in any form or by any means, including photocopying, recording, or other electronic or mechanical methods, without the prior written permission of the publisher, except in the case of brief quotations embodied in critical reviews and certain other noncommercial uses permitted by copyright law. For permission requests, write to the publisher, addressed "Attention: Permissions Coordinator," at the address below.

authorelsakurt@gmail.com
www.elsakurt.com

Ordering Information:
Quantity sales. Special discounts are available on quantity purchases by corporations, associations, and others. For details, contact the publisher at the address above.
Orders by U.S. trade bookstores and wholesalers. Please contact authorelsakurt@gmail.com or visit www.elsakurt.com.

Printed in the United States of America

ELSA KURT

WELCOME TO THE FAMILY

ELSA KURT

CONTENTS

CONTENTS iv
DEDICATION vii
FOREWORD ix
CHAPTER ONE 1
CHAPTER TWO 10
CHAPTER THREE 19
CHAPTER FOUR 24
CHAPTER FIVE 47
CHAPTER SIX 52
CHAPTER SEVEN 61
CHAPTER EIGHT 75
CHAPTER NINE 78
CHAPTER TEN 86
CHAPTER ELEVEN 93
RESOURCES 97
ABOUT THE AUTHOR 99

WELCOME TO THE FAMILY

ELSA KURT

WELCOME TO THE FAMILY

DEDICATION

To my buddy, my bruh, my friend, my husband, Paul. I like you and I love you.

ELSA KURT

WELCOME TO THE FAMILY

FOREWORD

I'm not an expert on anything but my own experiences. However, I've gained more knowledge through reading and listening to the experiences and advice of others and researching various aspects of police family behavior. My immersion in the police wife's life for the past thirteen years has granted me insights to the many facets of this lifestyle, of which I share here with you.

I don't pretend to be perfect, or to have lived an unblemished life. Quite the contrary. I've failed at marriage, made huge mistakes, and fallen flat on my face a time or twenty.

So, there are the negatives. While, yes, my fails have been epic in proportion, I wear their scars with pride. I've learned so much from those fails; the biggest lesson being the knowledge that nothing can hold me down for long. The second being that they make me able to help others avoid—or at least navigate through—their own misadventures.

More upsides: I have the joy of having raised two daughters, am currently succeeding at marriage, and am a prolific author, speaker, authorship coach, and brand designer, among other endeavors. So, although a degree doesn't endorse my opinions and suggestions, *experience* does. This isn't a one-size-fits-all book, but a common baseline many law enforcement wives, law enforcement girlfriends, and law enforcement significant others (from here on out LEOWs, LEOGs, and LEOSOs) find relatable by degrees.

The whole "not-an-expert" thing held me back from writing a police wife's life book... until now. It wasn't until this pesky pandemic changed our world back in March 2020 that I finally gave it real consideration. I'd been a published author for about eight

WELCOME TO THE FAMILY

years already—mostly fiction ranging from children's and young adult to contemporary fiction and romance—and did many books events over the years. Last year I developed my Path to Authorship coaching program, which was gaining traction. Things were going great. In fact, 2020 was well booked through October until Covid nixed every. single. plan.

I tried to bright-side my way through the first quarter. *Hey, I've been working nearly non-stop, great time to take a break*, I thought. But by May, I felt like my brain was atrophying. Then, in July—God help me—I discovered Tik Tok (@theotherelsa). I started making videos—anything, everything, all over the board—and began building a modest following. It wasn't until I made my first (of a series) of police wife life videos that I found my niche there. When my first one, a skit I called "Totally Normal Statements from Your LEO Spouse" passed 100K views and nearly eight thousand likes, I realized I'd found my tribe. And when I made my, "Types of Police Wives You Might

Meet," I knew I'd found the book I wanted to write. Sort of.

While we—LEOWs, LEOGs, LEOSOs—share the commonality of being involved with a LEO, our individual personalities, life events, and expectations are all over the board. Some of you are coming into this part of your life younger than when I did at age thirty-six. Some may have been with their LEOs before they were on the job, while others met them *while* on the job. You may be like me, coming into the relationship with children from a previous marriage, or you might be just starting out.

Even if I narrowed it down to just *Police Wife Life: Second Marriages with Kids* scenarios, there would be so many variations of what *that* looks like. In our case, my husband didn't have children, while I came into the picture with teen and pre-teen daughters, so that's way different from someone coming into the relationship with small children or someone with grown children, or from having both parties come into the relationship with children.

WELCOME TO THE FAMILY

Despite all the differences, we share realities the rest of the population cannot relate to or understand. Examples? A thought most people worry about on melancholy occasion—death, or the fear of—we collect rent from for the space in takes up in our brains every day. We know our loved one's work clothes—a source of pride, respect, and admiration for us—is a target for hatred and fear to others. Our cell phones are rarely out of reach. In no other profession—besides doctors and nurses, perhaps—do you always get introduced with, "This is Elsa, her husband's a cop." Sound familiar? Don't worry, it will soon enough.

These aren't complaints, mind you. Merely facts. But I'm preaching to the choir here, aren't I? If you're reading this, it's likely because you either already know, and are just looking for relatable content, or you're new to the Blue Family and need some reassurance that everything you're feeling and going through is normal. (Well, our version of normal.) You're in luck, honey. You found a place and space where it's okay to have all the feels, because we are right there with you.

Okay, so you've gotten the disclaimer, the background, and the slightly embarrassing knowledge about my Tik Tok obsession (which you *now* know is an obsession). The last disclaimer of sorts is to let my readers know that, while I consistently use the he/she and him/her pronouns and the terms husband and wife, it is solely for the sake of my convenience and nothing more. I view our LGBTQ partners, spouses, and family with equal affection and regard, and the following is for them as well. Also, everything in the forthcoming pages is generalized reflections of healthy relationships, and not the extremes.

Time to dive in. I do hope you find all the things I've tried to put in here—the humor, the relatability, the hard-learned life lessons, and most of all the love.

Xo Elsa

WELCOME TO THE FAMILY

WELCOME TO THE FAMILY

CHAPTER ONE

Types of Police Wives

If you skipped the Foreword, it's okay. No offense taken. There's a backstory to that chapter title. I'll just quickly explain it here, so you don't have to go back. I'm currently obsessed with Tik Tok. There, I said it. I own it. Among a billion other things, I make comedically intended videos about police wife life. One of them—with the above title—did pretty well and seemed to resonate with many of my followers. (Haters love to comment, too, but we'll get to them later).

In the video I portrayed six "types" of police wives: The Matriarch, The One Who

Makes the Rest of Us Look Bad, The One Who's REALLY Into It, the Second Wife, The One Who Doesn't Want to Know Anything, and the Shift Worker Who Doesn't Have Time For Any Bullshit. Going by the responses, I seemed to have nailed it. They also let me know what I missed, too. Like: The One Who's Never Around, The Gossip, The Rookie's Wife, The Military Wife, and the Liberal Wife. Since I'm wary of hurting any of my LEOWs feelings, I always do these in humor, without meanness.

The videos were easy to make because I embody variations of several of them, as do many of us. I'm in the matriarch phase because we're near retirement. I *am* a second wife. Clearly, I'm into it merely going by the videos, the children's book (My Blue Family), the clothing line (Blue Family Apparel) and this book. And yet, sometimes, I don't want to know anything. As for the shift worker, I know a few that I used as reference.

It should go without saying—but I'll say it anyway—that none of us are one-dimensional or can fit into a single category. My portrayal of the "second wife" is not representative of all second wives. The One Who Doesn't Want to Know Anything isn't uncaring to her LEO spouses' job or feelings, but understands that she needs to protect her peace to help restore his.

What it comes down to is this: whatever your "type" is, all that matters is that you support your significant other, you have their back—or in our world, *their six*. Embracing and adapting to this unusual lifestyle can only help you thrive in it. I believe the following pages should give you more than a glimpse at life behind the blue line and may help you decide if it is the life for you.

Partners not adequately prepared for the realities of this lifestyle often find themselves in a state of shell shock, wondering how the hell their sexy uniform guy turned into *third overtime in a week, sleeping all day/awake all night, sorry I have to work on Christmas* guy. This is often the case with the rookie couple. Sure, people told you stories. But hearing them and living them are entirely different.

I wish I could say that all the preparation and information you receive will make for smooth sailing. It won't. But it *will* send you in with open eyes. This is not an easy life. You never stop worrying, although you learn to live with it. Guns, tasers, handcuffs, duty belts, and sweat-stinky vests are all your normal. Flexibility is a must. So is self-sufficiency and independence. Understand that a police spouse's life will change you, but I believe it changes you for the better.

Is There A Typical Police Wife?

Only where they share some commonalities. Police wives are among the toughest people I know. I don't necessarily mean muscle bound, gun-toting Zena warrior types (we've got 'em, though). These are women who'll bake you a batch of cookies on Thursday, and on Friday they're hosing off blood-stained boots.

WELCOME TO THE FAMILY

They get woken from a dead sleep at three A.M. to, "Babe, I gotta go in. Shooting suspect standoff," and at six A.M., they're up and making breakfast for the kiddos as if nothing is amiss.

We are women who hear and see all yet say little. We are the shoulders to cry on for spouses who can otherwise never let their guards down. Generally, we hold ourselves to a higher standard with a different awareness—and wariness—of the world around us. When we break down, it's fierce and quick, then we're back to the business of life. We are anything but submissive or subordinate to our LE spouses.

The first time I realized how much I'd changed was at a concert with a group of girlfriends. Once upon a time, I'd enjoyed these things with little "situational awareness" and stayed content in my little cocoon of friends. Suddenly, I'm noting the exits and the best routes to get to them, scanning the crowd for anyone who looks "off," and making sure no one leaves their drinks unattended or goes to the ladies' room alone.

Since not everything is hearts and flowers, I'd be remiss to not acknowledge the other LEOW/LEOGs/LEOSOs who are less exemplary. Just like any group, you have your gossips, catty women, and the plain rude ones. You'll be stuck dealing with them—like at PD functions and gatherings—but otherwise, avoid them like the plague and don't get sucked into their vortex.

As a whole, we're a supportive group. If finding or connecting with your tribe locally is a challenge, consider joining any of the many online groups/pages on social media. The National Police Wives Association, your regional Behind the Badge chapter, and smaller groups like Wives Behind the Badge, are all great avenues to explore.

WELCOME TO THE FAMILY

Navigating the LEOW World

The most significant advice I can give you as you become more involved is to stay above the fray. Yes, it can be challenging. There is a lot always going on—relationship dramas, PD dramas, friendship dramas—and the wisest women are the ones who remain sympathetic but neutral. Always assume that engaging in gossip will bite you in the ass. Getting involved with someone's marital troubles will bite you in the ass. Picking sides in a wives' battle... you guessed it.

Oh, and keep your private life just that. It's no one's business what you and your spouse argue about or struggle with. Our spouses work in an alpha driven field, and if yours is trying to climb the ranks, the image you present as a couple matters. Competition can be cutthroat, so don't assume something you tell another LEOW/G/SO in private will stay private.

Rather, assume they tell their partner everything.

Everyone should have a trustworthy sounding board to vent to. Preferably, it should be your spouse. But that's not always the best option if you need objectivity. It's not uncommon to pose an anonymous question to the Facebook groups about your concern or problem. There are pros and cons to doing so.

Pro: Anonymity, multiple perspectives, and potential solutions.

Con: Multiple opinions, potential for detrimental advice, and the handful of know-it-alls.

I *do* think the pros outweigh the cons. Having a fresh set of eyes on something you're too close to see clearly from people who've been there, done that can be worth its weight in gold. I can say the same for the reassurance that you're not alone in whatever you're going through. Regardless of who or how you share your burdens or struggles, be sure to create healthy habits and strategies to cope with the many challenges of LE life.

Healthy Habits

- Making time to be alone together.
- Communicating honestly and openly.
- Setting ground rules.
- Having hobbies. (together and separate)

All the above sound obvious, I know. But life—especially a busy, chaotic one—can make us forget. I can't stress enough the importance of having time alone together. When you consistently make the time, the rest comes easily.

CHAPTER TWO

We Are Different

As if you haven't noticed, police wives are a different breed. We have to be. The *lifestyle* is profoundly different. You may lose friends and maybe even some family members. You will see the world, and the people in it, differently. Your "civilian" mindset—the one that feels safe and trusting—will become more guarded. Depending on what kind of department your spouse works in, whether he's city or town, and where you live, will only determine how fast or gradual that change is. But you will change.

Maybe change is too drastic a word. I know in my case; I've merely become *more* of who I've always been. As a long-time stay-at-home mom, raising my two daughters were my purpose in life. But as they matured, their needs for my time and focus diminished, while my nurturer tendency remained strong, if not unrecognized by me until I did some self-evaluating. As it turns out, I am someone who needs to take care of others, needs to always have projects and goals, and seeks a greater purpose in life. Cue a tall, handsome, gentle man with eyes that have seen more than most could fathom, a heart of pure gold… and BOOM. A new direction, just like that.

    I'm simplifying, of course. It wasn't really *just like that*. It was a gradual introduction, a slow immersion into a life that was completely foreign to me. I'd never dated a cop before. I had no comparison, no expectation, nothing to go by. Unless you count the stories people started telling me the minute I told them what my boyfriend did for a living. Ones that started with, "You know, cops are notorious cheaters…" and, "They're fun to look at, but a relationship with one? Yikes."

ELSA KURT

Forewarning: There is a lot of praise and expressions of blatant adoration for my husband forthcoming. I make zero apologies for the almost cringe-worthy love I have for him and our life together. He is that worthy of it. So, feminists and anti-romantics, put this book back on the shelf or return it to Kindle cyberspace if that makes you want to vomit.

Despite those generalized warnings, I took a leap of faith in him and treated each day and relationship milestone with a mantra of, "Things are great... so far." His one big task—regarding us as a couple—was to continue to be the man I believed him to be. I'm amazed to tell you that thirteen years later, he has never disappointed me. *Never*.

Now, without unpacking all the stuff and things, I'll say this is a *pretty big* deal. One that still awes me. Life experiences had taught me to expect nothing from anyone, and I'd never be let down. But in a relationship—a successful one—there *has* to be mutual, equal expectations. It's just how healthy relationships work. *I expect you to do these certain things. You expect me to do these certain things. I expect you to be a certain way. You expect me to be a certain way.* Lots of room there for failure, right?

I can't lie. He was the more emotionally evolved one of us. Thank God for his patience and freakishly intuitive understanding of what's inside my monkey brain, because the figurative chokehold I had on my feelings was life-threatening. Okay, fulfillment-threatening is more accurate. But I'm not exaggerating. Even saying, "I love you" properly—*I luh you. Iloveyou. Luh ya*—was a struggle. Don't worry, I've matured. If you ask him, he'd even go so far as to say I've grown exponentially.

My husband—wait, his name is Paul, so let's just call him by name from here on out—Paul has very sweetly likened me to a ferocious mama bear who fiercely protects her girls and him. I've always loved that he not only sees this quality in me, but cherishes it. The way he has shared his life and passion for his calling, his warrior perception of me, and his constant support and encouragement unleashed my need to live a purpose driven life. There is so much to say for a man who truly sees you, not only who you are, but who you can be.

Speaking of that warrior perception, I'm reminded of a favorite memory of a conversation Paul and I had once. We'd been talking about our previous relationships and I'd told him my ex had always seen and treated me like a princess, and even though I'd liked it in the beginning, I'd grown to despise it. He looked at me, puzzled, and said, "A princess? Nah. That's not what I see. I see a warrior." It was probably (and still is) one of the greatest things he's ever said to me.

I know I am not an anomaly in our LE world. The person we chose to love and who chooses to love us in return is a real-life superhero. Not the leaps over buildings (they would if they could) or laser vision (though it may seem like it to anyone on their wrong side) kind, but the kind who run toward danger, save lives, and make bad people go away. They are not your average humans, so it's a matter of course that neither are we.

Because of the unusualness of our lives, it can be challenging for us to relate to non-LEO people, and they us. All professions have value and worth and deserve respect. However, none—or extremely few—live with the low-key yet constant worry and knowledge that police families co-exist with. We don't outwardly make a fuss about it often; we just go about our lives. In that way, we're like everyone else. It's just that the things we worry, plan for, and discuss are jarringly... different.

Most of the time, you'll barely notice or care how different we are from them. It is typically only when a high profile OIS (officer involved shooting) occurs do otherwise innocuous people come out of the woodwork with opinions and views that we see their true feelings surface. It'll feel like a slap in the face when someone you've known for years, or maybe even a lifetime, comes out with some hateful blanket statement about police, but believe me, it's a blessing in disguise. I'd rather know who's against me and my family than be oblivious.

Between the Extremes

The one skill that will help you navigate this new life is learning balance. Balance is perhaps the most important tool in your box. You *absolutely* can balance the vastly different parts of your life. Civilian friendships and relationships do *not* have to fall by the wayside—unless they are anti-police—and police family life does not have to consume your existence. Don't get me wrong; it's going to take up a lot of real estate in your brain. A lot.

Paul gave me the best bit of advice early in our relationship. We'd been dating a few months and knew this was something special. He worked third shift back then, so I'd yet to see him in full uniform, so it was easy to pretend that what he did for a living wasn't "real." Then came a night where he worked a double and my kids were with their father, so he said, "Hey, why don't you come down and I'll meet you for a coffee."

I'd arrived first and was sitting when he walked in. There he was. Six feet of *damnnn*. I had two very distinct and contrasting thoughts. I sum the first up by that *damnnn*. The second was: Damn.

The reality hit me. The fear for him hit me. The understanding hit me. The person I'm falling in love with and see a future with will always be in the direct path of danger. Willingly. Running toward it. Once I had the image of me brushing my teeth and getting ready for bed while he strapped on a duty belt and answered calls in the middle of the night, I couldn't let it go. The worry flooded my thoughts.

I confessed them to him one night. I said, "Seeing you in uniform shook me. I realize what's at stake now, and I'm having a hard time managing the fear."

He said, "I get it. But we can't—*I* can't—let that fear rule me, and neither can you. If that happens, I can't do my job. You can't let it have that power over you, either. If we let fear of things out of our control, or that haven't yet happened, dominate us, we can't function. So, we compartmentalize. We put those fears in a drawer and close it. When we need to, we'll open that drawer, look inside for a bit, and then close it again. This is how we survive."

    I offer his advice to you. Acknowledge the fear; denying it will only do more harm. Put it in its box, let it out occasionally. But don't live there. What you can do is use it as a positive. Thanks to what they do for a living, we love deeper, hug harder, forgive faster, and live more passionately. At least we should. My loves, there is no time to hold on to anything negative when everything is so fleeting. I know, that sounds dramatic. But the older I get, the more I see... the more I know the absolute truth of this.

CHAPTER THREE

The Ups

Let's talk about the joys of police wife life. There are many to choose from, so I made us a list of my top ten.

1. For starters, we're part of something unique and incredibly important. It's more than okay to feel a swell of pride. Yes, they are the ones going out into the world to confront and handle the worst of society. However, we are the ones holding the line behind the scenes and keeping the home front together. They protect the peace on the outside; we protect it on the

inside. So, if you don't realize it yet, I'm here to tell you: you're a damn rock star. Never undervalue your role here... and no one else will ever dare.

2. We have a huge, protective extended family. Whether you're in a small town/small department, or a big city PD, your family has grown to over seven-hundred thousand brothers and sisters *and* all their family members. Help, understanding, and camaraderie is never further away than your phone. Police wives/partners/family groups on social media are easy to find. Some are great, others less so. Find the one that resonates with you and fosters a sense of community.

3. For as vulnerable as we may feel, we also share a sense of security. Sorry (not sorry) but there's just something about knowing your person can and will keep you safe if danger comes your way. Bonus security if you also carry, which is not uncommon in our world. Yes, I have my permit. For me,

knowing I can handle a gun if need be is a comfort.
4. Generally speaking (as most often throughout this book) we are tough as nails under our lovely exteriors. We rarely suffer fools, and we'll defend our LE spouses with the same ferocity we do our children.
5. Our bullshit gauge is finely tuned. We see people with new, more critical eyes than we did B.P.W.L. (Before Police Wife Life). This is not a bad thing.
6. We have impressive situational awareness. We spot the exits without even thinking about it, notice potentially suspicious behaviors faster, and avoid putting ourselves in situations that may be unsafe.
7. We rarely sweat the small stuff. Things that may have been a big deal in the past, simply matter less because our view of the big picture is unblurred. Please, I can't stay mad over a petty argument or a toilet seat left up.

8. We have a superior sense of capability. When our LE is pulling overtime or working nights, and shit needs to get done around the house... we get it done. Whether it means making the calls to get the faucet fixed or fixing the damn thing ourselves, we've got it.
9. We're independent. Goes along with number eight, just in a broader sense. When our LEOs work as much as they do, we learn quickly how to do things on our own. Yes, there are times when this sucks, so allow yourself a five-minute pity party, then pat yourself on the back for being a badass bitch boss who handles her business.
10. This one encompasses all the above: we are strong.

Consider this brief chapter your pep talk when things are rough. They will be rough at times, no question about it. In fact, at the time of this writing, we are collectively in the most challenging and scary part of policing that I've ever seen.

WELCOME TO THE FAMILY

Violent protests, anti-police groups, social media, the rabid mainstream media, and even an alarming number of politicians fuel an unjust firestorm of hatred toward law enforcement. These groups not only target police officers, but their families as well. Thanks to the internet, we are easier to find than ever. In the next chapter, we'll address ways to cope and manage this added stress.

CHAPTER FOUR

The Downs

Brace yourself. I'm ripping the Band-aid off: We're in dark times. It's been that way for some time now, and it's not ending anytime soon. The men and women *we* know to be good humans, loving partners and parents, and outright heroes, are being viewed by some of society as villains, murderers, and racists. These people hate the police, hate what they represent, and hate the people associated with them. They want departments defunded, police disbanded, and they want blood. They are being targeted for the uniform they wear, and we are under fire for standing beside them.

WELCOME TO THE FAMILY

This is even more reason for making your personal life—your home, your familial and friend relationships—a haven. It is imperative to healthy management of the external stressors to maintain a stable environment.

Home Life During Chaos

Pretending or denying we're living in the middle of a shitshow will only protect us for so long. All we can do is own the fear and worry, sometimes let it out of the cage and find a positive focus or outlet. Whether it's your own career, writing, volunteering, taking up karate, or starting a business, you **need** to channel and focus your energy on things that positively impact your life and give you purpose.

Understand that anti-police rhetoric is recurrent, and sanity will come back around again… someday. For now, we hunker down and wait. Remember, whatever we go through, we get through.

ELSA KURT

Regular Home Life

The reality of a police wife's life is that it can often feel lonely, particularly in the early years, and if your LEO chooses to climb the proverbial ladder. Holidays, special occasions, and even pre-planned date nights will be missed, canceled, and interrupted. My strong suggestion here—a relationship preserving suggestion—is don't give him hell for missing out. Yes, it's frustrating. Yes, it sucks to not have them there with you. But it is doubly so for him. Remember, *he* is the one missing out on the festivities, the memory making, the fun... not you.

This is not to say you should bottle your feelings or pretend it's all cool. "I'm sad you have to miss out today. I'll miss you," goes over a hell of a lot better than, "I am so pissed you're missing another get-together. This is bullshit." As my mother always says: It's not so much of *what* you say but *how* you say it. After years of failing at that skill,

WELCOME TO THE FAMILY

I've managed to at last master it (for the most part).

Ultimately, it serves us best to remember *this* is the life path he chose. *He* is the person we chose, and that means this is the life path *we* chose, too. Don't hold those choices against him. These are among the times he'll need your strength and support most and will be able to ask for it the least.

Practice the Pause

This simple skill spared many a fight that would have occurred because of my, ahem, over-reactive nature.

The first (and obvious) step is to pause before reacting. Sometimes that means literally walking away for a bit to work out all the immediate feelings. Say all the angry things in your head that you'd have said out loud. Next, think about what you actually want from him. Is it fair? Is it reasonable? Then consider where *he's* coming from and how *he's* feeling.

It doesn't make everything magically okay, but it *does* de-escalate the emotion.

Breaking Down the LEO Wall

Our LEOs, because of their job, come into nearly all their relationships with their guards up. Trust is a challenge, and it is fragile. In the development and growth of a healthy relationship, being the person he needs you to be will grow his trust in you *and* it will help him be the person you need him to be. That doesn't mean *pretending* to be the person he needs, but rather *understanding* what he needs.

Those needs are as simple as they are complex. He needs to know you have his back, that you understand the things he can't always say, and that he is safe to let that guard down with you. Being vulnerable is both their biggest desire and deepest fear. So, if you don't instinctively feel protective of that, the police wife's life is not the place for you.

If police life has been foreign to you up until now, the best suggestion I can give to you—besides reading this book, wink, wink—is to develop your empathy skills.

WELCOME TO THE FAMILY

Envisioning what he sees, does, and feels throughout a workday and relating it to how all those things might affect you, will foster and maintain a sense of compassion for him.

    Knowing his workday may have involved unsuccessfully trying to resuscitate a lifeless child, arresting someone who'd beat the crap out of their spouse, responding to a murder/suicide, or a fatal car accident is one thing. Sympathy causes you to say, "I'm sorry you had to deal with that." Empathy forces you to pause and really imagine what that must be like to hold a dead child in your arms or imagine your own rage at a man who beat a woman and how you'd have to use every fiber of your being to not kick his ass. It makes you picture the graphic, horrific sights of a murder/suicide and the gruesome image of mangled bodies inside wrecked vehicles. Suddenly, his inattentiveness during your planned romantic dinner isn't so annoying, right?

Conversely, having empathy doesn't mean you should live there, in that corner of his headspace. Allowing yourself to sink into that pit of despair and depravity will help neither of you. Someone has to bring the light into the darkness. There's a good chance he was drawn to *you* for your light, so don't lose that part of yourself. Keep your compassion forefront, and he will cherish you all the more for it.

Police Life

It's one of the few jobs out there that are way more than just a job. Most would deem it *a calling*. It's more than *what they do*, it's inherently *who they are*. Understand this, and you'll understand them.

We can say the same for police spouses. We're a different breed & we live a life that most can't imagine, let alone relate to. Even with the variations of our stories, the parallels outnumber the disparities.

WELCOME TO THE FAMILY

If your relationship began before he got on the job, you're likely to see a major personality change in him as he navigates his new life. It's going to take a lot of strength, patience, and understanding to navigate it with him. If you began dating him while already on the job, you have no point of reference for who or how he was before. The only thing you're likely contending with are preconceived notions and expectations based on what others have told you.

Regardless of how or when you met your LEO, adapting to the unique lifestyle will be a must. It won't adapt to you; it *can't*. Viewing the job as the time thief or attention whore in your relationship will only set you up for failure. You either swim with the current or get out of the ocean. *Drowning is not an option.

The Effects of the Job on Home Life

By the time my husband and I met, I was in my early thirties and he, his early forties. We were far from being a couple of bright-eyed kids unaware of the ways of the world. Despite my early attempt at ignoring the seriousness of his job, I knew better. Fortunately, because of our, *ahem*, advanced ages and life experiences, we came into the relationship knowing what it takes to fail at one. Neither wanted to fail again.

I also knew going in that this relationship would differ from any that came before. As a single mother of two teenaged daughters, I had zero time for games, drama, or bullshit. Been there, done that, too fricking old and busy for that nonsense. Paul was well-established and respected in his field, also older and wiser, and likewise had a zero-bullshit tolerance. In short, we were ready for each other.

Our first "rule" was that we both came in with a clean slate. Whatever roles we played in the demise of our previous relationships, whoever we were in those relationships, would not be held against us. We would not bring "baggage" into the relationship, but rather life experiences. Our conversations were open and non-judgmental. Yes, of course we failed at times. Fine, *I* failed at times. Okay, okay. I was a terrible communicator of feelings. It has taken me way too many years to be better at it. We've often joked that I'm "like a dude" in my inability to talk about feelings. All I can say is thank God he's a patient man.

A killer of relationships—as we all know—is a failure to communicate. If you block the communication airway, the relationship strangles. As much as I struggled with it, I knew I had to open up if this was going to work. The same applies to us all. To state the obvious, he needs to feel able to talk to you. You must feel able to talk to him. You both must be able to shut up and listen.

I warn you: you're not going to want to hear some of it. What they have seen, the things they've had to do, are all the things the rest of society is protected from. Human depravity, crimes against children and elderly, horrific, gruesome accidents, suicides, drownings, freak accidents… and on and on.

Odds are, he'll protect you and spare you from the majority of it. But there may be times when he needs to talk, and you'll need to let him. Even if it's a story he's told you before, maybe even many times. And even if it means you carry the scars of those stories on your heart right along with him. Consider it an honor and a gift when they share their burden with you, one that should never be taken lightly. If they're revealing their hurt, grief, anger, or helplessness to you, it's because they've put their faith in you.

In our LEOW group, someone shared that their LEO had an especially disturbing call and they wondered how best to handle it with them at home. Do they ask what happened? Do they push him to talk about it? Should they say nothing and wait it out? The answer, almost always, is this: Tell him you love him, you're so sorry he had to see and experience something so awful. He'll probably say, "Eh, I'm used to it. But thanks, babe," and that's okay. Say that you are always there for him if he wants to talk. With my husband I've said, "What would help you the most right now? Talk, silence, or distraction?"

Sometimes it's minutes, sometimes it's days, sometimes it's weeks or months later that they talk. Understand this isn't about you. It's about their need to process and compartmentalize. What they'll need from you is patience, love, and understanding. You know him best, so trust your instinct and not your insecurities.

Your Home, Literally

Welcome to duty belts, cuffs, keepers, and tons more on your kitchen table. Those pesky bullets will wind up in the washing machine along with mini notepads and pens. Uniforms, uniforms, uniforms. Oh, and from now on, you'll be receiving police related gifts and trinkets from everyone and you'll have to finds spots for them.

There are two types of police homes. In one, there's no mistaking who or what your family is. Blue Line flag waving in the breeze outside, a wooden sign (likely a Mathew 5:9) on the inside. Photos, trinkets, and décor throughout, all signifying this is a proud LE home and they don't care who knows it.

In the other, no one would know from the outside a cop lived there if it weren't for the take home. There might be a few small things here and there, but mostly, it looks like any other home interior. These are the ones who just want home life to be as normal as possible and/or fear being targeted.

There is no right or wrong here; both homes are perfect and need no justification or explanation. However, if you're in the first house and wishing for a little *less* thin blue line décor everywhere, perhaps encourage the man cave as the designated home for the excess. If you're in the second house and wishing for some *more* memorabilia, designating one room or area where only family is allowed may be a solution.

Friends & Family

I would be negligent to leave this part out: Your social circle will change. In a best-case scenario, you keep all your "civilian" friends, and gain LEOW friends. However, it is far from uncommon to lose some or even many of those non-LE friends. Sometimes it's blatant, in your face, "I can't be friends with you because you're with a cop." Sometimes it's a quiet drifting away. Sometimes it's them, and sometimes it's you. And sometimes, it's family you step away from or lose.

Losing (or leaving behind) people I believed knew and loved me because of my husband's career would have been unfathomable to be before this chapter in my life. Now, it's merely worthy of a one shoulder shrug and a Kardashian-esque, "*Byee*." I'm grateful when people show their true colors (or show themselves the door) because it saves me the trouble and wasted time. But that's just me. I decided long ago that I don't have to take shit from people just because "they're family."

For many, it's not so easy to let go of the hurt this causes, or to walk away from the people who cause the hurt. Only you can decide what's best for you and your mental health. If you can tolerate and accept those who don't support your spouse, manage to keep those two universes separate, and maintain those relationships... good on you, as the Australians like to say. I'm "not that guy," as *I* like to say.

While I can't give advice on how to maintain those relationships—mostly because I never have or will try to do so—I can help you get through the breakup of them. First: understand this isn't a *you* problem, it's a *them* problem. It's not your job to fix or correct their perception of law enforcement or police officers. The sooner you stop trying to explain shit to them they should already know, the faster you'll find peace.

Second: accept that if they aren't making your life better, you don't need them in it. Even if they are a blood tie. Seriously. Life is too short, too fragile to waste a single damn minute of it trying to fit square pegs into round holes. Surround yourself with people who understand, respect, and appreciate you.

Third: find and build your LE community. There is so much to be said for finding your tribe. Namely, the realization that you are not alone in anything you're experiencing. I say this to you as a self-proclaimed loner/introvert, by the way.

Can You Maintain Relationships with Police Haters?

Clearly, *I* cannot. I can "agree to disagree" on many topics. However, when it comes to the man I love, respect, and outright adore, you either support him and the profession, or you have no place in our life.

To be clear, this isn't blind adoration. We all know there are rotten apples in the bunch who need to be tossed. Good cops hate bad cops. When any of these highly publicized OIS cases come up in the media (then all over social media) I usually reserve stating my opinions until all the accessible evidence is out.

I've been asked, "Why so aggressive about it?" My answer is, "Because he puts **his life** on the line for you regardless of your feelings. That trumps all your misguided opinions."

And misguided they are. It takes little time or effort to research and separate fact from fiction, yet most people blindly accept whatever the mainstream media tells them. I have, many times, in the past tried to give them the facts—along with the sources for them to confirm for themselves—but few ever do.

As difficult as it may be, keep a cool head should you encounter these people.

They want to provoke you, so don't give them the satisfaction.

> **Comments & Responses**
>
> The things people say may never cease to amaze, but having a few pre-planned responses always helps.
> - Sometimes no response is the best response. Dead silence accompanied with an equally dead stare puts the spotlight back on them.
> - Most often, people have no facts to back their unwelcome opinion. Ask them to site their sources or to explain themselves.
> - End the conversation with, "This isn't something we're going to agree on."

Mainstream Media

Although we can't entirely avoid watching/ hearing/reading the news—nor should we—it's in the best interest of our mental health to limit what we consume. We're long term in part of the cycle where "good guys bad, bad guys good" according to the media. The good news is that most of the population doesn't agree. The bad news is that the ones who *do* agree are the louder voices.

While I like to use my platform to advocate for our LEOs—remember, most often they cannot do so—whether *you* choose to engage in the conversation in a public way is up to you. There's no right or wrong, as long as your LEO knows you support him. At the end of this book, I'll have some great resources to reference when correcting misconceptions (or outright lies). I've found them invaluable both for my understanding and for straightening out the misinformed (although, asking them to site *their* sources usually shuts them up quick.)

Acquaintances & Strangers

As you can probably guess, I care even less about these people and their opinions. Don't get me wrong—they affect me. I'm a fighter by nature. You know the saying, *"I don't start them, but you can be damn sure*

I'll finish them?" Yeah, it's like that. Especially if you come at someone I love. Hell hath no fury like a mother… or a police wife.

As I've mentioned, we are living through an unprecedented period of anti-police rhetoric. Certainly, we've seen it before—tied typically with politics—but never so bad as it is now. We can sarcastically thank the mainstream media for this, who sensationalized recent cases and perpetuated the myth of widespread police brutality against blacks.

Simply put: the facts do not support the rhetoric. However, getting people to understand this is often a futile effort. While I choose to arm myself with these facts to hammer away at them, you are under no obligation to do the same. I do feel that having the knowledge in your arsenal is valuable, if only for yourself. See the info box at the end of the chapter for some fun facts.

People can and will talk shit as if they have a damn clue. Spoiler: most of the time they don't. This especially applies to social media, where keyboard warriors and basement dwellers virtually congregate. You'll have to choose between suffering fools, or not. Regardless, don't let them under your skin… much. And when you do, be sure to kill em with passive aggressive, fact laden kindness and then walk away.

Social Media

Whether you love social media or hate it, most of us use it regularly. If you're a public figure and run an online business like me, you probably need it, too. Regardless, it's the ultimate frienemy, and how you navigate it matters. It's easy to forget this from behind a keyboard.

Generally, we keep our personal profiles—meaning our posts, pictures, and even friends list—set to **Friends Only** and often use only our first and middle names for our usernames for the sake of privacy and safety. No matter how few or many online friends you have, always treat it as if anyone can see it. What you say and do on there can have a lasting and negative impact on your LEOs career, not to mention your family's safety.

Whether you use social media or not, there's a strong probability your friends and family members do. You'll need to make clear whether you are comfortable with them sharing news and photos of you, your LEO, and your children. Most people are respectful, but some can be outright belligerent and even dismissive. Stand your ground if you feel strongly and let them know the consequences of not respecting your privacy.

This could be as simple as saying, "I know it's hard to imagine, but there are people out there that may want to cause us harm, so keeping our personal life private is very important to us." If they push or ignore your wishes, then you may have to tell them you may not be able to attend functions or visit with them in the future if they can't take your family's needs seriously. Again, this is about what your family needs to feel comfortable and safe.

Fun Facts

There are approximately 700,000 sworn LEOs in the United States.

Annually there are approximately 53 million encounters with police, resulting in approximately 10 million arrests.

95% of whites and 85% of blacks said police acted properly during encounters. Only 2% claimed force or threat thereof.

While a 2019 NAS study found that "people of color face a higher chance of being killed by police" it failed to account for confounding variables.

Source: Law Enforcement Today article by Jeffrey James Higgins.

CHAPTER FIVE

Our Normal

So, all the above? That is our normal. Everything abnormal to others, is normal to us. Also normal:

Christmas/Thanksgiving/Easter a day or two early or late. Never getting to face the door in a restaurant. Finding bullets in the washing machine. Calling his work friends by their last name. Sleeping with your phone beside/on your pillow. Being asked if your LEO can "help me get out of a ticket." Explaining that your LE spouse really exists, he's just working. Blackout curtains. Being asked, "Can you see it now" before leaving the house in civilian clothes. That he takes two showers a day. Leaving restaurants before you order, because turns out he arrested the cook last week. Those aforementioned duty belts, cuffs, and more on your dining room or foyer table. Gallows humor.

It's amazing and amusing how fast abnormal becomes normal. The best advice I can give is roll with it. Seriously. Don't fight it or attempt to change it, just accept and adapt. This doesn't make you a Stepford wife, it makes you a team player. Conversely, this doesn't make your input, feelings and needs invalid. But if you're going to fight things that are inherently part of the lifestyle, you're in the wrong place.

They're Not All the Same, But...

They have... similarities. A lot of similarities. So, pardon the stereotyping/generalizing. It's a given that their work personalities and home personalities are different. All you have to do is talk to him on the phone while he's in the PD to hear it. My husband is fond of saying, "Go, Unit," when I call him while he's inside (Yes, I roll my eyes every time) compared to the, "What's up, babe," outside the PD.

To state the obvious, when they're on the job, they present a certain way. Stoic, in control, wary. It's like a second skin. Sometimes, or maybe often, it's hard for them to peel off that skin when they come home. Guess who's job it is to remind them, "You are not on the job right now, honey"? If you raised your hand, you win.

Some find it difficult to drop the Alpha attitude and need to run the show at home. If you're cool with that, good on you. Otherwise, you may have to remind him you're neither a subordinate nor a criminal in the back of the cruiser, so watch the tone. They're not even aware they're doing it. The few times Paul has slipped, I've said, "Pardon? Who are you talking to like that? Because I *know* it's not me," and we laugh.

Conversely, some LEOs, when they are home, don't want to be *that guy*. It's fairly common for them to defer to you on most home related decisions, planning, and managing of your day-to-day life. This has the potential to be frustrating, especially if their at-home behavior seems outright lazy or disinterested. In our home, my husband is the primary financial provider. I handle the home front. If I worked outside the home, I'd expect an even split of responsibilities. Everyone's situation is different, so my best advice is to be fair and realistic... and pick your battles because some will never end!

About Alphas

The notion that Alphas are macho, bossy, mark their territory types is a misconception. A true alpha is easy to spot. They are the ones others look to for leadership, advice, and guidance. They are usually agreeable and very easy to work for and with!

His Normal Isn't Like Other People's Normal

WELCOME TO THE FAMILY

Their "normal" behavior/personality may be the one you've always known, but a closer inspection will show you the underlying causes for just about everything they do. For one, they are never *not* in LEO mode. Not even when they're asleep. When in crowds, they're always scanning. Same for restaurants (where he sits facing the entrance), movie theaters (where you always sit in the way back) and just about anywhere you find people. Accept it, appreciate it, and get used to it.

Understanding the *why* of how your LEO behaves will help you as much as it does him. As I mentioned earlier, the best way to do that is simply imagine what he sees, feels, and experiences. Remember, empathy is your greatest friend when married to a LEO. They are like icebergs in the ocean; what we see above the surface belies what is below. You are of the few who see below the surface.

CHAPTER SIX

The Not-So-Normal

The stresses of police life take both a physical and emotional toll on our LEOs. Sometimes—like in the examples in the previous chapter—it's obvious. Other times, it subtle and almost undetectable. Again, they operate at a level that is only normal in their world. So, when is the already-not-normal too far from, ahem, normal?

Mood swings that seem to come from nowhere, inability to control emotions, distancing behavior, and any behavior inconsistent with the person you've known them to be are all warning signs that something is amiss. It may be tempting to "wait it out" and sometimes this is not only acceptable, but necessary. Trust your instincts (not to be confused with your hormones). If it feels wrong, it's probably wrong. Don't be afraid to ask or even push if you're truly concerned.

An unfortunate side effect of their natural ability to compartmentalize, is that they may mask depression or anxiety with more ease. This is *way* harder to detect under the "everything is under control" projection. It is so important to establish yourself as his safe space (I hate that catchphrase, but it applies here). That means he can come to you to talk, and he can come to you for quiet. When in doubt, ask him what he needs from you.

Odds are, he's not going to tell you he needs help. He won't ask for it. There's a good chance he'll go straight for the, "I'm fine," response that they're pre-programmed to say. Talking it out is not natural for them, and in their job, admitting to emotional strain is not only a sign of weakness, but can even be career damaging or ending.

Knowing their reality makes it apparent how and why they bottle everything inside. For us, it's even more reason to show compassion, patience, and understanding. Don't try to change this about him—insisting or demanding he talk to you—it's a battle you're bound to lose and push him further away in the process.

Our biggest mistake in dealing with our spouses is our absurd expectations of them to see everything the way we do. What is so fricking obvious to us is mind-boggling to them. Trust me, the four hours we spend dwelling on how he did or didn't say good morning has not taken up an ounce of real estate in his brain.

Asking him how he couldn't understand something that is plain as day to you is like asking someone who *literally doesn't speak your language* to understand what you're saying. So, what do we do?

Start with acceptance and expect it in return. It's okay that he doesn't comprehend why you get so mad over something he views as trivial. (Seriously, we get so obsessed with being *understood* when all we actually need is acceptance.) Their man brain only understands what they deem as logical. Therefore, saying, "You don't have to understand. You just have to accept that this is how I feel about this," is much more likely to get a sympathetic response.

Likewise, accepting *his* way of expressing things and what he responds best to, is your key to helping him. Saying, "I *need* you to open up to me," is likely to make him shut down more. He already has enough people always needing things from him. You're the safe space, remember?

He *does* owe it to you and the relationship to communicate. This isn't an area where we give free passes for shutting out the person who *is* their person. However, making him feel cornered or pressured has about the same effect on him as it would on you.

You know your man best. Where and when is he most comfortable and at ease? What does he respond best to? Learn his "love language" and you both win the battle. There's a renowned book—The Five Love Languages—out there about this. Totally worth checking out.

Hopefully, these tips will help avoid reaching a point where his normal becomes a concerning not-so-normal. When in doubt, it's always okay to seek outside help or advice from a professional.

WELCOME TO THE FAMILY

> **My Favorite Phrases**
>
> Yes or no questions don't invite conversation. Asking, "What can I do for you?" or "How can I best help you right now?" is a better opener than, "You need anything?"
>
> When I know it's been an especially hard day, I'll ask, "Would you like silence, conversation, or distraction right now?"
>
> The empathy alone will matter most to them. Don't worry so much about saying "the wrong thing," just say *something*.

But What About You?

There's a saying I really love: *You cannot pour from an empty cup.* I can't express enough how important it is to take care of *you* foremost. If you are drained and exhausted, worried sick, and stressed to the point of breaking, and still giving, giving, giving... stop. Being a martyr will never serve you well.

Believe me, I'm not saying you're *trying* to be a martyr. I'm saying the bullshit advertisements and general messages that we should, "never quit," and that we can handle anything and everything thrown our way, that we never surrender or back down, never let them see you sweat... just *ugh*. That stuff is fine for brief spurts, but for life advice? No. Shut it right the fuck off.

Calling time-out or acknowledging fear, or—*gasp*—weakness is *not* admission of defeat or failure. It's *humanity*. Having a place to vent or burn off steam is vital. So, don't bottle your feelings to spare him. Pick a regular time and place to just get everything out there. Paul and I have a regular, weekly date night. It's just the two of us, our favorite restaurant, plus some amazing martinis. Our conversations go anywhere and everywhere, and it's our reset button from a long week. We both feel reconnected, heard, and reassured that even though the rest of the world is crazy, we're still okay.

WELCOME TO THE FAMILY

Soapbox Moment

One more thing about taking care of you. I mentioned my love for that empty cup saying, but now here's one I hate: *You complete me.* Or—just as bad—*you're my everything.* Ladies, please. I am begging you. Do not put him at the center of your universe. Nor should you be the universe to him. Romantic love should **not** be unconditional.

I'm sorry to tell you this, but the fairytales, romance novels, and movies all sold a lie and an illusion destined to create failed relationships. People who believe they are broken cannot be "fixed" by another person. If you want a fulfilling, healthy relationship complete/fix your damn self and expect the same of him. Love and respect yourself first, and no one will dare otherwise. Love with the expectation that it's conditional; meaning, you each toe the line and act right or else. Understanding you could lose the person you love because of your destructive behavior is different than fearing you'll lose them because of your insecurity. One comes from emotional maturity, the other, immaturity.

Sorry to be harsh about it, but that really needs to be the foundation. Obviously, no one is going to always be their best self, and you need to give each other room to grow, allow space for forgiveness, and accept one another for who you inherently are. A couple with a strong base can do those things with little trouble because the two individuals that make the couple are self-confident, mature people who recognize their own shortcomings and have a willingness to work on them.

WELCOME TO THE FAMILY

CHAPTER SEVEN

The Cringe-Worthy

Yes, there is plenty of cringe-worthy stuff. From their overly graphic work stories, to inner PD dramas, police groupies (AKA: Badge Bunnies) and more. In this chapter, we'll try to cover—or *un*cover—those major ones mentioned above.

The work stories. Oh, the work stories. Not all LE spouses share the gory details, but a lot do share *some* of them. And when I say gory, I mean blood gory, brain spatter gory, things you can't mentally unsee even though you didn't *actually* see it gory. What I can tell you about those stories is that they aren't sharing them with you because they find them entertaining or funny—even if they're laughing a bit when they share—they're telling you because they need to purge the horrors before locking the memories away. Let them tell the stories.

There's a good chance you'll hear those stories over dinner, too. We've discussed incidents where a man blew his brains out with a shotgun over appetizers, how another man was stabbed to death and folded into a storage container to rot between ordering another round, and the volume of blood at a scene while enjoying dessert. He has taken calls while out at dinner about a suicide victim hanging in the woods, an elderly man burnt to a crisp on his porch, and more. This is the reality. It's ugly and sad, and often horrifying. Until you've become used to it, it'll—rightly—seem morbid. One way they (and we) cope is called gallows humor. It means dealing with the grim or hopeless with grim and ironic humor. It's a defense mechanism that's almost a pre-requisite for survival.

PD Drama. There is always cringey PD drama, always a story to tell. Someone's always getting written up. Someone's always getting divorced, and it's almost always ugly. There will be someone cheating on someone else. Someone leaving the job unexpectedly. On and on it goes. The rule is, if you want to be privy to everything, say nothing. Be the keeper of secrets, not the gossip—yep, every PD has one—and you'll never *be* the story.

Speaking of stories—but only as a cautionary tale—I know of a former LEOW who not only spilled the tea about a LEO from another department, but unwittingly spilled it to the LEO's wife. It was a mortifying situation for all involved, and a hard lesson learned. Moral of the story, if it seems like gossip, don't say anything about it. Even if—*especially* if—asked. Chances are, if you're being asked what you know, you're being either tested or played.

LEO and LEOW socializing often has a quiet undercurrent. It's impossible to not be aware of the hierarchical order in your spouse's department. Patrol typically hangs with patrol, sergeants with sergeants, admin with admin. When all mixed together for larger gatherings, everyone is tip-toing to some degree.

It's not to say we don't have fun together, because we do. However, it will always serve you well to remember there are lines to not cross. The Lieutenant's wife is not going to discuss a patrolman's recent reprimand with patrol wives (not that she should be discussing it at all). A patrol wife is not going to trash talk a sergeant to a sergeant's wife (again, not that she should be discussing it at all). Do not be the reason your LEO is spoken to because *you* spoke out of turn and ruffled feathers.

Police Groupies. There are a few names for these special little pop tarts. Badge Bunnies, Holster Sniffers, Holster Humpers... you get the idea. They're after any man in uniform and don't care if he's yours. In strong relationships with secure males, they're annoying but laughable. If your husband/future husband has that damn Peter Pan Syndrome, he's ripe for the picking. My suggestion? Be very clear in your zero-tolerance stance. This isn't about control, it's about respect and it runs both ways.

Thanks to the above, LEOs don't really love bringing their girlfriends/wives around their coworkers, who—not wrongly—have a reputation for being hound dogs who will sniff around anything that moves. I recall shortly after Paul and I started talking, I told my girlfriends that he was a cop. The immediate reaction from some was, "Ooh, a cop? That's hot." And from others, it was, "Oh, *no*. You know their reputations, right?"

Between the women who single-mindedly pursue cops and the cops who are very receptive to being pursued, it would seem us spouses/significant others have our work cut out for us, hm? Well, hold up. Just because there is a percentage of *them*, there are also plenty of do-right guys, too. Not only have I married one, but I also know many who have, too. Allow me to stray slightly from the strictly cop wife life stuff for a few paragraphs...

ELSA KURT

Our Formula for Success

The dynamics of every relationship is different. I would never presume that our way is the only way to have a successful one. I know couples who've done everything the opposite of us, and they've been married way longer with no signs of calling it quits. The following is merely what works for us. If we have the type of relationship that appeals to you, then this will give you the nuts and bolts of how we created it.

Early on, Paul and I put not only our concerns and reservations, but our respective expectations of each other out in the open. We laid out all the obvious must-haves—respect, trust, honestly—and then dug into what those things mean to us. We learned not only the *how* of the way we each do/handle things, but the *why* of it, too. Having both come from failed marriages, we knew what we didn't want and were old enough to have no problem stating it.

I know the above sounds like we were exchanging job applications rather than falling in love, but for us, it signified *this is different*. This is *special*. Neither wanted to fail again, neither wanted to waste time treading water with someone who didn't fit our lives. Having said that, I can assure you, there is no lack of passion, excitement, or attraction between us. In fact, it is all deeper thanks to our profound understanding of one another. If I were to sum up the magic ingredients of a successful relationship, I'd use the formula Paul coined: Timing, Chemistry, and Balance. Each one on its own isn't enough. Two out of three isn't enough. It has to be *all* three.

Timing. You could take the two most *they'd-be-perfect-together* people, put them together at the wrong time in life, and they'll fail. Example: Paul and I agree, with little doubt, that if we'd met at our younger versions of ourselves, we'd never have made it. The attraction would've been there—he's *everything* I find attractive, and he says the same for me—but he was Type A, climbing the career ladder and fully immersed in the police life with hardly any time to devote to a relationship. I was headstrong, stubborn, and selfish. Plenty of chemistry, but no balance and bad timing. But flash forward a handful of years, and here we are, the milder, gentler, more evolved versions of ourselves.

Chemistry. This one is the most fun. It's the intangible, the static electricity thing between two people. It's the thing people always talk about when excited over a new relationship. But without balance and at the wrong time, it's temporary. If you look back on failed relationships you might say it was all fire and passion in the beginning, then it just fizzled out. That's because for chemistry to last long-term, there must be more than just static electricity and heart-flutters.

In our first year together, Paul and I took a weekend getaway trip to a small resort lodge in New Hampshire. It was our kind of perfect—rustic, serene, romantic, and even better, the room had a small sitting area with a fireplace—and just what we needed. The drive had been long, and we agreed to unwind for a bit before heading out to explore the area.

We each sheepishly pulled a book from our bags, half expecting the other to scoff—it was a romantic getaway, after all—but instead grinned and cozied up on the couch. For an hour, we quietly read our books together in front of the fire. Paul, being the more sentimental of us, said, "This feels like a moment. Like, a memorable moment. There's something special about being able to be comfortably quiet with someone."

He was right. It's still a favorite memory after all these years. What he was pointing out, really, was that it's easy to be happy and in love when you're doing things and going places—it's all excitement and fun—but being *still* together is a different kind of special. It shows you who you are or can be when the novelty of early love morphs into every day, settled love.

Balance. As much as trust, respect, and honesty are the foundation of a strong relationship, balance is the glue that holds everything together. If either or both of you can't balance out the work and home life, you'll struggle. If either or both of you are unbalanced emotionally, you'll struggle. Too much or too little in any form for too long will tip the scales too far.

While I feel this is the basis for *any* romantic relationship—not just LE relationships—I stress the importance for LEOs/LEOWs because of the unusual external strains put upon us.

Police Life: A Breeding Ground for Discontent

It's my opinion that no one can come between a happy, strong marriage. If one or both are unfulfilled or unhappy, there is room for someone else to fill the gap. That's not blame throwing, just facts. To be clear:

WELCOME TO THE FAMILY

Cheating is the fault of the cheater. Period. Yes, circumstances may have led to the act, but the act is a choice.

Can you insure it will never happen in your relationship? No. There are no guarantees in life. But you build the foundation and create a life together where you put each other before everyone else, make the effort to stay connected, compassionate toward one another, and truly be best friends, then you've got one hell of a shot.

For our LEOs, their work world is adrenaline and testosterone fueled. Extreme ups and downs, high and low-key stress, and pressure. Uncommon schedules. Unrelatable (to most) lifestyle. This leads to a tendency to stick with those who understand their lifestyle. So, if you can't understand it and assimilate to it, chances are you'll be on the outside looking in. And if your LEO feels disconnected from you, he'll connect with someone else.

That doesn't necessarily mean he'll cheat. Not in the traditional sense, at least.

The connecting may mean more time out with the boys off-duty. Having a "work-wife." More separate activities than ones together. Maybe this works for you—and that's fine—but for me, it's a hard no. I didn't get married to be alone, and alone is how I would feel if our life were like that.

LEO's tend to get a bad reputation for the above, but LEOWs are no angels, either. Long periods of being alone leads to feelings of loneliness, as can feeling disconnected to that side of your spouse's life. Those feelings lead to resentment, and resentment leads to trouble. Many a shitstorm has started because of going outside the marriage for companionship or validation.

Conversely (and a bit ironically) excessive involvement in the PD life is a potential battlefield, too. The tendency to become friends with other LEOs breeds a inclination toward familiarity, and familiarity can lead to line-crossing in a vulnerable marriage. Anyone alive longer than a hot minute knows the sharks can smell blood in the water, and they will absolutely move in for the kill if the opportunity arises. For the love of God, don't be fooled by an offer of a sympathetic shoulder to cry on. Also, no one—not one single person—believes the, "Oh, my God he's just being nice," thing.

This goes for social media bonding, too. The best way to protect your marriage is to keep your business off those platforms. Airing your dirty laundry tells the sharks you're vulnerable, which translates to a seemingly innocent DM to "check if you're all right." I've seen it happen. If you do choose to "vent" on social media, just remember it's out there forever.

Social Media

Department rules vary, so make sure you know what yours allows. Pictures of your LEO in uniform may be a no. Photos or posts about drinking may be frowned upon, too.

Often, LEOs & LEOWs set their privacy to "Friends Only" and don't use their last names. This is not solely to stay off criminal's radar. Every small town seems to have a group of vocal anti-police citizens who'd like nothing more than to "bring down" the LEOs who work there, and their first line of attack is trolling the accounts of both LEOs & LEOWs. Don't give them an opportunity.

There's a line between being outspokenly supportive and antagonistic or confrontational. As much as we'd like to go for the figurative jugulars of those vocal against our LEOs, it gives them fuel to use against them. Use discretion and caution when fighting those battles in public forums.

WELCOME TO THE FAMILY

CHAPTER EIGHT

Finding the Humor

I mentioned our gallows humor—which is almost a pre-requisite for balancing out the madness—but having a plain old good sense of humor will take you far as a LEOW. We tend to take a lot more in stride than most, mainly because we choose to not sweat the small stuff. By the way, most things are small stuff. Let's face it, when you're sending your spouse off to a job where he could get seriously injured or worse, and where he may have to injure-or-worse someone else, that toilet seat lid that is never put down isn't worth mentioning.

Let me state a contradictory fact: Hell, yes, seasoned LEOWs lose their shit over small stuff, too. Our tempers flare, we give them hell for something or other, and sometimes we want to kick their damn ass... just like every other spouse out there. For example, if someone could please explain to me why, for the love of God, does he put his balled-up napkins in his glass and his trash on the counter above the trashcan cabinet??? Anyone? Sigh. We are not always *so* different, after all.

When we get together with our "regular wife" friends, the pet peeves become a universal bonding moment. Sure, the civilian wives look at us sideways when—after they complain about the toilet seat thing—we say, "Ugh, I know. If I have to take his duty belt off the dining room table one more time..." Or, "Right? I'm so sick of fishing bullets out of the washing machine..." but it's all good. We laugh, they laugh... nervously.

Finding humor amid chaos and craziness is a skill, and if you've found yourself in a relationship with a cop, you probably already have it. Marriage and family minded LEOs tend to seek life partners who can handle the lifestyle and get the humor (or at least accept it). However, if you're just pretending to get or accept it and then try to squash that trait, you'll cause way more harm than good.

Gallows humor is not a habit like nail biting, but a critical coping tool. The truth is, if they don't find ways to laugh, they'll cry. That goes for us LEOWs, too. The precariousness of that balance is one thing that is no joke. Understanding and accepting at least this much—even if you don't like or partake in it—is enough. Believe me, there has been the one or two occasions when I've had to stop my husband and say, "Oh, whoa, nope. Too far for me, sorry."

There will be plenty of times when they or we won't be able to find the humor. Sometimes things get plain dark. So, lean into the moments of laughter—inappropriate or not—and know that it is a vital part of LE life that most people can't relate to (and may be horrified by) because it's part of what gets everyone through the madness.

CHAPTER NINE

Weathering the Storms Together

Even with all the tips, insights, advice, and figurative tools in your box, storms will blow through your life. All the things that happen externally—in the PD, across the country, politically—will be absorbed to some degree. Establishing the ground rules of your relationship helps you weather the storms together.

Establishing Your Relationship Rules Early

1. Know and be clear about what's acceptable to you. Anything outside the normal scope of his professional duties (this includes the inevitable and frequent overtime) needs to be on the table for discussion. For example,

if his having an off-duty friendship with a opposite sex co-worker is an issue, say so. If it's not acceptable to you, it's not acceptable, period... unless that friendship existed long before you came around.
2. Determine who handles what at home. As I mentioned earlier, it's not uncommon for LEOs to have little interest in the day to day running of the household. Others are micro-managers. What works for *you*?
3. Does he need to leave the alpha dog mentality at work? Tell him so. Yes, he needs to be told because he probably has no idea he's doing it.
4. If you expect to be his person—the one he unburdens to and shares with—let him know. Because if he's not talking to you, he's bottling it all or talking to someone else.
5. Finances, future goals, kids, retirement. Yes, they should all be discussed.

Every great relationship is built on a solid foundation that you create as a couple. The only blueprint for success is the one you design together. It doesn't matter if *I'm* fine hearing them, you can have a limit to how far he can go into detail for some of those work stories. You can't be his rock if you're traumatized.

Certain things, like PD drama are a standard across the board: Don't talk about anything you're told. As for groupies—and anyone else trying to come between your marriage—set those ground rules in stone and leave no room for misinterpretation. When you lay it all down early, it leaves no room for confusion or misunderstanding.

In our home, we established a few basic rules.

1. Home is the haven. That means all the drama, the bullshit, and negativity from other people isn't welcome in our home. It's not to say we're unsympathetic or uncaring, even though it may sound like we are. We just have boundaries and limits to how involved we'll get.

2. It's us against the world. We are a team, a unit, a combined force. We are stronger together than apart. I have his back, and he has mine. Always.
3. If someone gets in either of our lanes, handle it. This can refer to a number of things, like someone shit-talking him/police to me when he's not around, or someone hitting on either of us. I trust he'll shut the crap down, and he trusts the same with me.

For us, and many LE couples, it boils down to protecting our peace. The world can be as crazy and toxic as whatever, but inside our bubble, the air is pure, the water is smooth like glass, and the sun is shining. Sounds like a fairytale, I know. But thirteen years in, I can tell you, it's our reality.

We built our life on that strong foundation of honest, open conversations, mutual understanding, shared visions and goals, and daily effort to maintain and nurture the relationship. This doesn't mean we are clones of each other, though.

It's comical how different we are in some ways. He's thoughtful and deliberate; it takes him forever to commit to something, whereas I'm impulsive and have no problem jumping face first and even failing. He's more sensitive and demonstrative, I'm… much improved at expressing feelings. He's patient, I'm not.

Yet it is also eerie how alike we are. Fiercely loyal to those who've earned it. Introverted. Artistic/creative. Stubborn. Determined. Patriotic as hell. Music/concert lovers. Wary of people. And so on. But our biggest shared traits are our sense of boundless gratitude and our need for peacefulness.

Together, we've weathered several life storms, and we know there will always be more to come. However, there is peace in trusting we can weather them together because we've proven we can. When people say marriage is work, it's not a bad thing. It means not taking the other person for granted, being truthful about who you are and what you want and allowing the other person to be who they are.

I realize the above can apply to any relationship, as it should. Secure, balanced people gravitate toward secure, balanced people who in turn surround themselves with the same, raise the same, and encourage the same in others. In LE relationships, it's that much more critical to strive for balance and peace at home, as it directly impacts their work performance.

If you were to take a superficial glance on the internet for the divorce rate amongst LE couples, you'd read that over sixty percent of those marriages end up in divorce. The claim is also that domestic abuse, suicide, heart attacks, and alcohol abuse are also elevated considerably. Those are disturbing percentages, right? Well, hang on. A deeper delve tells us not only are the studies outdated, but they are also subjective.

To my knowledge (yes, this means I could be wrong), there are no updated, reliable studies to confirm these stats. What *is* accurate, is that policing presents a host of potential problems unparalleled in other careers, and therefore could more easily lead to negative vices and behaviors. Hence, all the above tips, advice, and encouragement. LE life does not have to equal a guaranteed marriage fail. I know many successful, long term LE marriages, and I've witnessed LE divorces.

Usually, it's one of (or a culmination of) these issues:

1. He's changed since becoming a cop. This is common lament amongst LEOWs/LEOGs whose spouses became LEOs after they married/began dating. There is some serious decision making here. Change with him, adapt, and embrace this new version? Fight for what was? Walk away? As I've said before, this lifestyle isn't for everyone.
2. Long-time married couples whose children have flown the nest. Also sadly common, and why it's so imperative to

continuously work on staying connected as a couple. Raising a family is time and energy consumptive, and it's easy to put each other on the back burner. Just remember who's left beside you when the kids move on.
3. Infidelity. The biggest trust breaker of all. Yes, there are marriages that have survived this. Mine would not, because I would not allow it. No judgement if you choose to move past it (should it happen). I just know what I can and cannot accept.

> There is no fail-proof formula. I wish I could say there was. You could do all the things, give your whole heart, and still fail as a couple. The best thing you can do for yourself and your marriage is love yourself first, respect yourself, and be clear on how you expect to be treated. Then, reciprocate.

CHAPTER TEN

Red Flags

Let's start with dating red flags. I think it's a given that we all want to believe the best in people, especially people we love. Unfortunately, that need to believe can blind us to truth about them, too. When you're in the thick of a new relationship, it's easy to overlook or disregard those red flags that are telling you something is off.

Peter Pans

Peter Pan Syndrome—the inability for a man to grow the hell up—is common. It's also easy to recognize when you're looking for it. When combined, the following are tip-offs: inability to commit, obsession with his own physical appearance, never letting you look at his phone, and never sharing your relationship status/pictures of you together on social media are solid indicators he's a dud. You won't change him, so spare yourself the anguish.

Here's the obvious: Peter Pans never man up. To them, settling down with one woman means they'll miss out on all the fun of single life. Some more tip offs he's a Peter Pan: He refuses to give up his excessive bro time, and the gym will always be a huge priority and time suck. His incredibly buff bod is, ahem, enhanced. Oh, and he probably has a racing bike. Sorry, but this is the vanity starter pack.

Bored Guys Looking for No Strings Fun

No strings because he's already married, that is. Make sure he's not married. If he says, "it's complicated" and he's leaving her, walk away. Sure, that might be legit, but unless he can concretely prove it to be true, you're asking for heartbreak. That line is as old as time. Tell him he can find you on Facebook when his divorce is final.

If he says he *is* divorced, it's easy enough to check (public records), so check. That doesn't make you a psycho, it makes you cautious. If he says he's single, there's no valid reason to never go to his place unless you don't want to). After you've been seeing each other for several months, there's no good reason to never meet his friends or family, for him to have two phones, or for him to see you only at specific times or days, and never on his days off.

If you're banned from the PD or bringing him a coffee while he's on duty, I'd be wary. The same goes if he has a reputation. If you can't ever post anything about him on social media (he doesn't want anyone "in his business," or some other excuse) then I'd be suspicious.

WELCOME TO THE FAMILY

Narcissists, Control Freaks, and Other Assholes

Unfortunately, policing can attract a certain type that is contrary to what they are intended to represent. It's more than unfortunate, it sucks. For every thousand well-intended LEOs, you get a handful of shitbags who use the title and their power to dominate, manipulate, and control others. We despise them.

The Control Freak. Some tip offs on this type are they often pull out all the stops to impress you. Big romantic gestures, early declarations of love, more than happy to meet your family and friends. So attentive and sweet you think he's almost too good to be true. Sigh. He *is* too good to be true.

The shift is subtle, then increases. A misunderstanding—*that guy was hitting on you. No, he was just asking the time*—becomes a regular thing. You miss his call, and he's miffed. You cancel a date because of a family thing, and it becomes a fight—

you don't love me. The friends he liked in the beginning are all against him—*they're jealous of how much I love you.* On and on like this until it's just easier to not do the things that piss him off. It'll only get worse.

The Narcissist. What starts off looking like self-confidence in the beginning soon shows itself for what it really is: and over-inflated sense of importance. He expects you to fawn all over him, then sulks or picks a fight when you don't give him adequate attention or affection. He's forever got big plans and ideas that never seem to come to fruition. The promotion he had in the bag goes to someone else, as does the commendation, or otherwise mark of success. He's wholly unsympathetic to anything you're going through. He's arrogant and petty. You're constantly on high alert for his moods. They are skilled gaslighters.

> **Gaslighting**
>
> Gaslighting is a type of psychological manipulation with the goal of gaining power over someone.
>
> Narcissists and sociopaths use gaslighting to make their victims question their sanity. This kind of emotional abuse causes the victim to feel a sense of loss of identity and worth.

The Other Assholes. I mean, let's just call it what it is. An asshole is an asshole. He's demeaning and rude, he probably has touches of both the above two guys, and he flakes out on things that are important to you. You're with him because you think deep down, he really does love you, and/or you can change him. Stop, honey. You can't. Go back and read all that stuff about loving and respecting yourself. Then dump his loser ass. Don't fall so in love with the idea of the man, that you don't see him for who he really is. Please. For your own sake, get those blinders off. I don't have to know you to know you deserve so much more than what they can give you.

For as often as the stresses of the job are acknowledged and discussed, it is never,

ever a justification for mental or physical abuse. Policing—as much as some would like you to believe—is not synonymous with domestic abuse. An abusive person has likely been an abuser their whole teen/adult life, and unless they get serious psychological help, they will remain abusers. Facts: There is no excuse in the world great enough to justify abuse. You/your love cannot fix or change them. If they hit you once, they will hit you again. Verbal abuse is abuse and may be a precursor to physical abuse.

If you are in an abusive relationship, there is help and support for you in every state via **National Domestic Abuse Hotline 800-799-7233**.

CHAPTER ELEVEN

The Nutshell

My primary goal here was to pack as much useful information in the most straightforward manner. I'm not a big fan of long-winded anecdotes or taking forever to get to the point. I also wanted to make clear, then often reiterate, that this book was written from the perspective of someone in a strong, healthy relationship for others in/looking for similar circumstances.

I next wanted to share all the wonderful parts of police wife life—the honor, privilege, and pride of it—to offset the negatives. For all the bad things associated with LEO/LEOW life, the good outweighs them. That's my opinion, at least.

We could chase our tails all day long trying to get those determined to hate law enforcement to see the good, but—ultimately—what matters is that *we* see it. As spouses and partners, we are in some ways their advocates and protectors. This may seem ironic—the protectors needing protection—but they do. It's our job to protect their peace as much as our own.

Inevitably, someone will read this book and suggest I sugar-coated the harsher realities of life behind the blue line. More accurately, the intention is to uplift, inspire, and encourage my fellow LEOWs/LEOGs. So, I limited the downsides to acknowledgements and brief passages. This is not a denial of their existence. There are many books out there that delve deeper into the psychology of police family life, should you wish to learn more.

There will also be those who—much like my handful of social media trolls on Tik Tok—think that because I talk about and advocate for police wife life, I must be using my husband's job for "clout" and that my identity is so tied up with being a LEOW that I don't have my own. To them, I say... nothing. I don't care enough about their opinions, nor do I feel any need to justify myself. I do what I do for those who can or want to relate.

I mention the above for those who see themselves taking on a vocal, active role in the LEOW world. The haters will always crawl out from Mommy's basement, from under their rocks, and their little troll bridges to harass you. Generally, it's best practice to simply delete and block. Believe me, they are not looking to have their minds changed or to have an intellectual conversation. Admittedly, I'm not above the occasional troll-back. Especially on Tik Tok. But generally, I ignore them.

For everything I've written here, and for everything you'll hear and read from others, you'll still need to create *your* version of success. Whether you become highly involved in the LEOW life, or stay on the peripheral, all that matters is building your life together, protecting each other's peace, and staying connected. Trust me, your tribe is always around should you need it because—ready or not—you're part of the family.

WELCOME TO THE FAMILY

RESOURCES

There are many books, articles, groups, and websites to help you navigate this unique lifestyle.

Books:

Emotional survival for law enforcement: A guide for officers and their families by Kevin M. Gilmartin

Cuffs & Coffee: A Devotional for Wives of Law Enforcement Paperback by Allison P. Uribe

The Five Love Languages: The Secret to Love That Lasts by Gary Chapman

Websites:

Law Enforcement Family Resources - Law Enforcement Family Resources | International Association of Chiefs of Police (theiacp.org)

Law Enforcement Today Law Enforcement Today - Your source for cutting-edge law enforcement articles and information

ELSA KURT

Article:
Higgins: Enough Of the Lying Higgins: Enough of the lying – just look at the data. There's no epidemic of racist police officers killing black Americans. | Citizens Journal | Citizens Journal

Groups:
National Police Wives Association
Wives Behind the Badge
The Wife Behind the Badge

ABOUT THE AUTHOR

Elsa Kurt is author of more than twenty books, ranging from her children's books—including My Blue Family—and young adult, to contemporary fiction and her non-fiction guide, Navigating the Path to Authorship. In 2019, Elsa developed her coaching program, Path to Authorship, to help new and aspiring authors pursue and achieve their authorship dreams.

In addition to writing, Elsa is a speaker and brand designer of iGoodhuman, Blue Family Apparel, and Very Sweary Stuff. All of Elsa's links can be found here: https://linktr.ee/elsakurt. Find Elsa across social media as @authorelsakurt and @theotherelsa and at elsakurt.com.

www.ingramcontent.com/pod-product-compliance
Lightning Source LLC
Chambersburg PA
CBHW021115080526
44587CB00010B/531